Animals in the Wild

Turtle and Tortoise

by Vincent Serventy

RAINTREE
STECK-VAUGHN
L I B R A R
A Division of Steck-Vaughn Company

Turtles and tortoises are closely related
reptiles. Most have hard outer shells.
Turtles use their flippers for swimming.

Tortoises usually live on land or in fresh water. They have legs rather than flippers. The largest are four feet long.

The largest turtles are giant leathery
turtles. They grow to about ten feet long

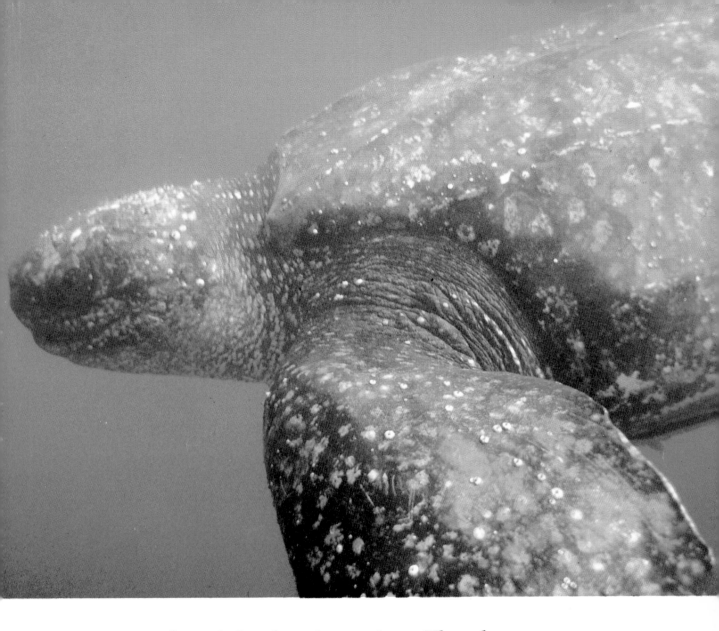

and weigh about one ton. They have no
outer shell, only tough outer skin.

Green turtles live in most of the seas of
the world. They grow to over three feet

long. Green turtles like to play during the mating season.

Green turtles eat sea grass and algae.
Scientists put metal bands on the legs of
turtles that they want to study.

Loggerhead turtles have larger heads than
other turtles. They eat crabs, fish,
mollusks, jellyfish, sponges, and seaweed.

Animals like barnacles often attach themselves to turtles to travel. Female turtles lay their eggs on shore.

The females come ashore at night to be safe from enemies. They come at high tide so that they don't have to travel so far.

Moving on land is hard work. The female
finds a spot above the high-water mark

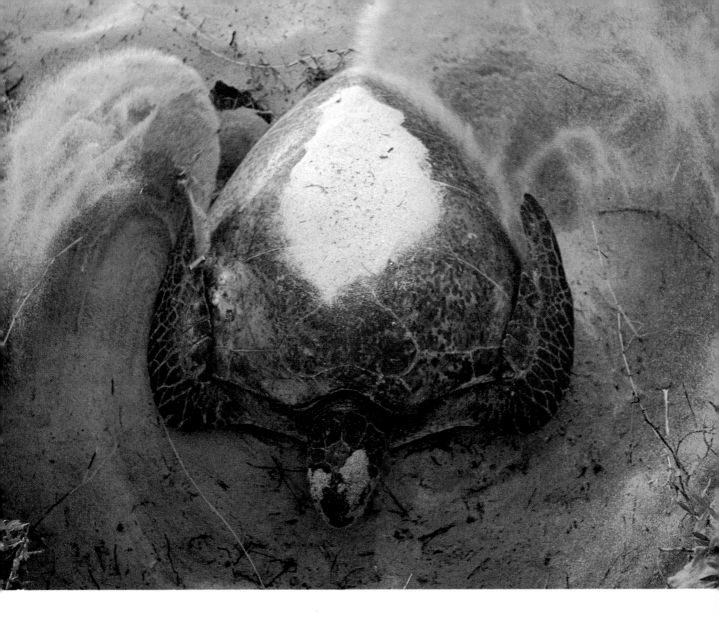

that has no roots or stones. She digs a
huge nest in the sand with her flippers.

Then she digs a nesting pit with her hind flippers. She lays many eggs in it. The eggs have a tough skin and look like ping-pong balls. She fills the pit with sand.

14

The female covers the nest so that
enemies will not be able to find it. Then
she heads back to the water. Usually the
tide has gone out, and the sun is rising.

The eggs hatch a few months later. The
tiny turtles dig toward the surface. They

usually dig out of the sand at night and head straight for the sea.

Freshwater tortoises are close relatives of
the sea turtles. The tortoises live in rivers

and lakes. They eat meat—mostly fish,
pond insects, and snails.

Turtles and tortoises use their shells to protect themselves when on land. They

pull their legs and heads into their shells,
which are very hard.

Giant land tortoises eat plants. They can be found in forests in some parts of the

world. Where tortoises have no enemies,
they have become very tame.

First Steck-Vaughn Edition 1992

First published in the United States 1985
by Raintree Publishers, A Division of Steck-Vaughn Company.

Reprinted in 1987, 1989

First published in Australia in 1984 by
John Ferguson Pty. Ltd.
133 Macquarie Street
Sydney, NSW 2000

The North American hardcover edition published by arrangement
with Gareth Stevens Inc.

Acknowledgments are due to Vincent Serventy for all photographs in
this book except the following:
Vedat Acikalin p. 3; Ron and Valerie Taylor p. 4–5, 7, 9.

Library of Congress number: 84-15881

Library of Congress Cataloging in Publication Data

Serventy, Vincent.
  Turtle & tortoise.

  (Animals in the wild)
  Summary: Describes the life cycle and natural environment of the turtle
and the tortoise with emphasis on their struggle for survival.
    1. Turtles—Juvenile literature. [1. Turtles]
I. Title. II. Title: Turtle and tortoise. III. Series.
QL666.C5S4   1984   597.92   84-15881

ISBN 0-8172-2403-3   hardcover library binding

ISBN 0-8114-6891-7   softcover binding

5 6 7 8 9 10 11 12 13   99 98 97 96 95 94 93 92

DATE DUE
